PROJECTS

How to Bake a CAKE

Anastasia Suen

Rourke
Educational Media

rourkeeducationalmedia.com

*Scan for Related Titles
and Teacher Resources*

Teaching Focus:
Concepts of Print: One to One Correspondence- Point to each word as you read.

Before Reading:

Building Academic Vocabulary and Background Knowledge

Before reading a book, it is important to set the stage for your child or student by using pre-reading strategies. This will help them develop their vocabulary, increase their reading comprehension, and make connections across the curriculum.

1. Read the title and look at the cover. *Let's make predictions about what this book will be about.*
2. Take a picture walk by talking about the pictures/photographs in the book. Implant the vocabulary as you take the picture walk. Be sure to talk about the text features such as headings, Table of Contents, glossary, bolded words, captions, charts/diagrams, or Index.
3. Have students read the first page of text with you then have students read the remaining text.
4. Strategy Talk – use to assist students while reading.
   - Get your mouth ready
   - Look at the picture
   - Think…does it make sense
   - Think…does it look right
   - Think…does it sound right
   - Chunk it – by looking for a part you know
5. Read it again.
6. After reading the book complete the activities below.

Content Area Vocabulary

batter
gooey
mitts
spatula
toothpick
yolk

After Reading:

Comprehension and Extension Activity

After reading the book, work on the following questions with your child or students in order to check their level of reading comprehension and content mastery.

1. *Why is it important to let the cakes cool before frosting them?* (Infer)
2. *Before making the batter, why should you heat the oven?* (Summarize)
3. *What is your favorite kind of cake?* (Text to self connection)
4. *Why is the toothpick test important to do?* (Asking questions)

Extension Activity

For birthdays in the United States we usually eat cake and have a party to celebrate. Is this the same in other countries? Research birthday traditions or celebrations around the world. What did you find? Do other countries celebrate differently?

Table of Contents

Let's Celebrate!

A big day is coming. You can make it a special day. You can bake a cake!

⭐ **Ask an adult to help you.**

4

You will need:

baking spray

2 ½ cups (625 milliliters) flour

2 cups (500 milliliters) sugar

4 eggs

1 cup (250 milliliters) milk

¾ cup (175 milliliters) vegetable oil

2 ¼ teaspoons (11 milliliters) baking powder

1 teaspoon (5 milliliters)
  vanilla

measuring spoons

measuring cup

spatula

mixing bowl

electric mixer

two 9-inch (23 centimeter) round baking pans

oven **mitts**

cooling racks

Oven and Pans

First, put the oven rack in the middle of the oven. Then turn on the oven.

Heat the oven to 350 degrees.

Let the oven warm up while you make the cake batter.

Spray both cake pans.

Always wash your hands before you start cooking.

You don't want the cake to stick to the pan. Coat it with cooking spray before you put in the batter.

Make the Batter

Put the sugar in the mixing bowl.

Now add the eggs, one at a time.

Tap the egg.
Then crack it open.
Pour out the **yolk**
and the white.

Turn the bowl as you mix.

Turn on the mixer.

Mix the ingredients for one minute.

Now, add the flour, oil, and milk.

Add the baking powder and the vanilla.

Use a spatula to scrape the sides of the bowl.

Now, mix everything together.

Use the mixer again for one minute.

Make the **batter** smooth.

Bake Your Cake

Pour half of the batter into one pan. Then pour the rest of the batter into the other pan.

Tap the pans to pop any air bubbles.

If one pan has more batter, it will take longer to bake.

Wear oven mitts so you don't burn yourself.

Put the pans into the oven.

Bake for 30 minutes.

Is your cake ready?

Test it with a **toothpick.**

A toothpick will let you know if the inside is baked.

If the inside is still **gooey**, put the pans back in the oven. After two minutes, test the middle again.

Did the toothpick come out clean?

Then your cake is ready.

If it did not come out clean, bake it a little longer.

Take the pans out of the oven.

The pans will be very hot! Wear oven mitts to take the pans out.

Use a thin knife to loosen the cake from the pan. Then flip the pans over onto the rack.

Put each layer on a rack.

Let them cool down.

Decorate Your Cake

Now you can frost your cake.

Frost the middle first.

Then frost the top and the sides.

Use a knife to add a big scoop of frosting. Then spread it out.
Repeat until the whole cake is covered.

Slice and serve your cake!

★ You have made it a special day!

Photo Glossary

batter (BAT-ur): A mixture of milk, eggs, and flour used to make cakes.

gooey (GOO-ee): Something that is sticky or soft.

mitts (MITS): Padded gloves that protect your hands.

spatula (SPACH-uh-luh): A tool with a wide, flat blade that bends.

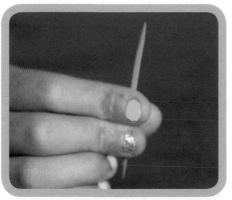

toothpick (TOOTH-pik): A small, thin piece of wood.

yolk (YOKE): The yellow part of an egg.

Index

Websites to Visit

www.food.com/recipe/simple-vanilla-cupcakes-178370

www.womansday.com/recipefinder/the-very-best-vanilla-cake-recipe-122339

www.dvo.com/recipe_pages/bestloved/Bonnie_Butter_Cake.html#.Upj4ptJDu3J

Meet The Author!
www.meetREMauthors.com

About the Author

Anastasia Suen baked her first cake when she was in second grade. Her daughter baked her first cake in preschool. Mrs. Suen lives with her family in Plano, Texas.

www.rourkeeducationalmedia.com

PHOTO CREDITS: All photography by Lisa Marshall Photography except: page 5 © Ljupco Smokovski/shutterstock; page 6 shutterstock: © Laurin Rinder, Jeffrey B. Banke, Coprid, Nagritsamon Ruksujjar, Hurst Photo, Andrey Eremin, Sheila_Fitzgerald, Warren Price Photography; page 7 shutterstock: © sevenke, Dancestrokes, Reload Design, endeavor, Petr Novotny, Kitch Bain, VikaRayu, Crepesoles; page 22 shutterstock: top © phloem, middle © Madlen, bottom © VikaRayu, page 23 shutterstock: top © Reload Design, bottom © Kanomjeeb

Edited by: Keli Sipperley

Cover design and Interior design: by Nicola Stratford
www.nicolastratford.com

Library of Congress PCN Data

How to Bake a Cake/ Anastasia Suen
(Step-By-Step Projects)
ISBN 978-1-63430-357-6 (hard cover)
ISBN 978-1-63430-457-3 (soft cover)
ISBN 978-1-63430-555-6 (e-Book)
Library of Congress Control Number: 2014934360

Rourke Educational Media
Printed in the United States of America, North Mankato, Minnesota

Also Available as:

ROURKE'S e-Books